CW00644339

Copyright © 2013 Momeni & Jones

All rights reserved. This book or any portion thereof
may not be reproduced or used in any manner whatsoever
without the express written permission of the authors
except for the use of brief quotations in a book review.

First Printing, 2013

ISBN 978-3-00-044641-2

ultimateguidetocelta@gmail.com

The Ultimate Guide to CELTA

Amanda Momeni & Emma Jones

Contents

Preface

The aim of this book is to help you prepare for the challenges that lie ahead on your CELTA course. There is a chapter for each part of the CELTA syllabus and within each chapter you will learn from the trainees' experiences about how to deal with potential difficulties.

The authors of this book survived CELTA and each went on to build a successful teaching career. Now, as experienced trainers, they help numerous participants through the ups and downs of their courses.

The illustrator's drawing abilities came to light on a CELTA course. She is now a qualified and practising teacher.

All characters appearing in this work are fictitious. Any resemblance to real persons, living or dead, is purely coincidental.

Meet the Trainees

Harassed Henry

Hi, my name's Harassed Henry. I'm married to Pleasant Pat and have two children, aged six and nine. I've recently taken voluntary redundancy after 15 years working in insurance. I've hardly spent any time with my children, and feel like I've missed out on too many of their early years. I've got enough redundancy money to keep the family afloat for a year, but definitely need to get some work, sooner rather than later. I've decided that I'd like to have a go at teaching English as a foreign language. Although I don't have any teaching experience, I've done some training sessions in previous jobs, so think that it's something I'll enjoy.

Fastidious Felicity

Hi, my name's Fastidious Felicity. I've been with my fiancé, Jolly John for 2 years; we're getting married at the end of this year. I was a straight 'A' student at high school and at college, and have been a volunteer for various charity organisations since leaving school. I trained as a high school teacher in the US, but then met Jolly John, and we moved over here with his job. For the past year I've been working as a secretary in a law firm, but I don't find the job challenging enough. I've decided to take the CELTA course because I know I'll love teaching - both my parents are teachers so it must be in my blood.

Chilled-out Charlie

Chilled-out Charlie

'I stumbled into it really.'

Hiya, I'm Chilled-out Charlie. I spent a few years after university travelling and did a spot of teaching to keep my head above water while I was abroad, so I stumbled into it really. I seem to have settled here for a while, and now have a few classes. All my students tell me they really like my lessons and have a lot of fun. I thought I'd give CELTA a go, as it seems to be the qualification all the schools ask for.

Anxious Annie

Hi, my name's Anxious Annie, I've just left university, and have decided to take the CELTA course. I've always been fairly shy, but I can't believe how nervous I am about teaching. I know I'll be able to overcome these nerves, in the same way that I did in the past when giving presentations at university. It's not the students I'm worried about, I just don't like the idea of being watched and judged by other people.

Anxious Anne

'I'm anxious about being watched!'

Course Content

Harassed Henry (HH) is talking to Pleasant Pat (PP) about the course he would like to apply for:

HH: It sounds really interesting, and if I get the CELTA Certificate, I'll be able to start teaching straight away.

PP: So, what do you do on the course?

HH: Well, apparently I'll have to complete six hours of assessed teaching practice.

PP: You have to actually teach on the course?

HH: Yes, it's a practical course. Anyway, isn't it better if I practice teaching before I am let out into the real world?

PP: I suppose so. But how will you know how to teach?

HH: Well I hope they're going to tell me.

PP: Let's just hope they don't get you teaching straight away.

HH: Actually, I read somewhere that I could be teaching as early as Day 2 of the course!

PP: OMG!

HH: I'll also have to complete four assignments.

PP: Well that'll be OK, you're not bad at writing

HH: Yes, but I imagine the content is quite important!

PP: It sounds like *you* have to do all the work - teaching practice, written assignments and who knows what else. What are you actually paying for?

HH: There will be various input sessions delivered by the tutors; I guess this is when we learn the theory before putting it into practice. We also have to observe experienced teachers, to see how it's done.

PP: Well, experienced teachers aren't always the best. Remember that Spanish teacher I had last year, she was awful! But, I suppose if you're lucky and you observe someone like my current teacher, Popular Pablo, then you'll be OK.

HH: It looks like there's a lot of support on the course. The tutors help you with lesson planning and give feedback on the teaching practice - I just hope they're nice when giving feedback.

PP: I'm sure they will be, they must have been through it themselves. So how long is the course?

HH: The one I'm interested in is a four-week course, apparently there's a minimum of 120 contact hours but I'll be expected to do about another 120 hours outside the course.

PP: That sounds like quite a lot of time but I suppose it'll be worth it in the end if it means we can spend more time together as a family. So, what are you waiting for? Send in your application!

To pass the course:

- Six hours assessed teaching practice per candidate, supervised by a course tutor.

- Six hours observation of lessons, taught by experienced ELT professionals, up to three hours of which may be on DVD.

- Four assessed written assignments.

What the course consists of:

- A minimum of 120 contact hours

- Input sessions, covering topics such as classroom management, lesson planning, teaching skills lessons, language awareness.

- Tutorial support and consultation.

- Supervised lesson planning.

- Six hours of observed and assessed teaching practice.

- Feedback on teaching practice.

- Peer observation of teaching practice

- Approximately 120 additional learning hours for pre-course preparation, reading, research, assignment writing, lesson preparation and record keeping

NB. 100% attendance is necessary to pass the course (in case of emergency, work must be made up in the trainee's own time)

Getting Accepted

So you've decided you'd like to do a CELTA Course. You've probably thought long and hard about it already, but just take a little more time before you apply, and ask yourself these questions:

☑ Am I fully committed, and able to dedicate 100% of my time to a full-time course?

☑ If it's a part-time course, am I available for 100% of the course?

☑ Do I live near enough to the centre to get to the course and back home again, still with course work to do in the evenings and at weekends? If not, where am I going to stay during the course? Can the centre help me with finding accommodation if necessary?

☑ Do my nearest and dearest realise that they will have to help me through this, by feeding me regularly, being a guinea pig when I need one, and then allowing me sufficient time and space to study and prepare?

☑ Do I have the necessary equipment to complete the course? It wouldn't be advisable to embark on a CELTA course without possessing a computer and a printer; in fact many centres will insist on it

☑ Have I ensured that my children will be taken care of, even if they're ill?

☑ Have I got the funds to pay for the course? Most centres will want the money to be paid in full on registration.

☑ Have I got the PC skills to manage basic programmes, such as Word?

The Application

Harassed Henry has a look at the centre's website but doesn't have time to read it all through carefully, so is unsure how to apply. Rather than taking the time to read the information provided, he decides to write to the centre with a long list of questions.

Anxious Annie takes time to read the centre's literature, and finds out all she needs to know about the application process, the price of the course, the start dates, and so on. Once she's sure that she has all the details, she completes her application and sends it to the centre.

Fastidious Felicity also takes the time to read the information provided, but she does have a question to which she can't find the answer, so she sends an email to the centre before sending her application. She emails her application as requested by the centre and also mails 25 certificates of various achievements, including her Grade Six trumpet exam, which she feels might help her cause.

Chilled-out Charlie, like Anxious Annie, has completed his application but he isn't available for a face-to-face interview on the scheduled dates, so he calls the centre to see if this is a problem, before sending in his application. He is told that a VoIP or telephone interview can be arranged, so he sends in his application.

All four candidates get through the application stage, but Harassed Henry and Fastidious Felicity have started off on the wrong foot. Henry has demonstrated his lack of meticulousness and Felicity has been over-enthusiastic in her application, causing the centre extra paperwork to deal with.

Be careful! On receipt of an application, (this includes the cover email) there are a few things that a centre will be looking out for:
- Can the applicant communicate well in English?
- Does the applicant make any spelling or punctuation mistakes in his/her application?
- Has the candidate done what he/she has been asked to do?

The Language Awareness Test

Before the day of the interview, Fastidious Felicity brushes up on her knowledge of the English language. She does some research on the internet, and asks friends who've already completed the course about which books she should look at. She makes sure she knows the basics, such as what an adjective is and the names of the tenses.

Chilled-out Charlie doesn't worry too much about the language awareness test. He knows that he's aware of the language, so what is there to prepare for? He is, after all, a native speaker, so surely he knows his own mother tongue.

The kinds of things that are tested in the language awareness test are:
- Meaning and form of language
- Describing language
- Contextualising language
- Lexis & Phonology

Experience shows that native speakers do not generally know much of the terminology used to describe language, and many are not sure what an adverb or an auxiliary verb is. This gives non-native speakers an advantage at this stage in the application process, as they tend to have learned many of these labels when they learned English. Getting a really low mark in your language awareness test will prevent you from being accepted on the course, however, places are not offered based solely on this test.

The Interview

Chilled-out Charlie makes a good impression at the interview stage. Although he sees the teacher's role as that of an entertainer in the classroom, he deals well with the language awareness questions, and is able to suggest an appropriate classroom activity for practising how to order food in a restaurant. The interviewer believes that he would be a useful contributor in feedback, and is sure that the "performer" side of him can be sorted out.

Harassed Henry interviews well. He knows exactly why he wants to do the course; he wants a job with more flexibility, as his wife wants to go back to full-time work, and they have 2 children. Plus, he was so bored with his office job that he decided to take voluntary redundancy. He feels he'd be much more suited to working with people. He gets slightly worried as the interviewer asks him whether he's cleared his diary for the month of the course. He doesn't have any other commitments as such, but he knows his wife will still expect to be able to go to her Spanish evening class and Zumba. However, he pushes that thought to the back of his mind; "surely the course can't be *that* intensive, can it?"

In her one-to-one interview, Anxious Annie struggles to keep her nerves under control. She informs the interviewer that standing up in front of a class fills her with trepidation, but she's working on her nerves, and is sure that she'll be able to handle it. She does very well dealing with the language questions the interviewer asks; thank goodness she did a lot of preparation before the interview.

In the one-to-one interview, you will probably be asked a couple more language questions such as "How would you explain the difference between a bachelor and a spinster?" The interviewer will be interested in your language learning background, as well as why you want to do the course, and how you will cope with feedback. Assuming you are applying for a full-time course, they will also want to know if you have cleared your diary for the four or five weeks of the course.

Checklist

☑ Do I know anyone who's already done the course, whose brain I can pick?

☑ Have I checked my application for language mistakes?

☑ Have I reviewed grammar basics, such as tense names and uses?

☑ Do I have any questions I want to ask in the interview?

☑ Why, exactly, do I want to do the course?

Preparing for the Course

Chilled-out Charlie knows that the next four weeks will be pretty intensive, or, at least that's what he was told at the interview, but, he wonders how intensive it can really be. He's done a degree, so he knows how much work goes into studying; This course can't be more intensive than his final weeks at uni, can it? To prepare for the weeks ahead, Chilled-out Charlie decides to have a final blow-out with his mates. He has a big night out on Saturday, and then spends the majority of Sunday watching wall-to-wall sport. He forgets to check the shopping list given to him with the pre-course task, so doesn't have any of the materials he was told to buy before the course began. He'll have to do that in his lunch break tomorrow. Surely he won't need these things right from the start? He wants to go to bed early, but he suddenly remembers that there was something he should've done before the start of the course, so he wastes valuable sleeping time trying to work through the pre-course task.

Anxious Annie's a little more careful about her pre-course preparation. On Saturday, she goes to the supermarket, and stocks her cupboard with all the foodstuffs she needs to keep her energy levels up. She knows that she won't get much chance during the course to fill her pantry, she just hopes there'll be some time during the week to pick up fresh fruit and vegetables, and get some fresh milk for the numerous cups of tea she'll be consuming. She then goes to the stationery shop to get the rest of the items on the course shopping list. On Sunday morning, Anxious Annie packs her bag ready for the next day, and then spends the rest of the morning reading through all the pre-course literature to make sure she's done everything she was asked to do before the course begins. She has a nice relaxing afternoon with some friends, safe in the knowledge that she's well prepared for the beginning of the course. She goes to bed early on Sunday night, puts her mind at rest by going through everything one last time, and then sleeps like a baby.

It is important that you begin a CELTA course fully refreshed and raring to go. As the start date draws near, it is advisable to fill your sleep bank as much as possible. Avoid having a busy weekend before day 1, you may come to regret it. There will be nights during the course when you will find yourself staying up until way past bedtime, trying to complete a lesson plan, or cutting up bits of paper for an activity - this is when you will be drawing on your sleep bank, and will feel pleased that you didn't go hard at the weekend.

Checklist

- ☑ Have I bought everything that the centre requires?
- ☑ Have I completed the pre-course task?
- ☑ Have I got ahead by brushing up on my language awareness?
- ☑ Have I caught up on sleep?
- ☑ Have I got enough food in the house?

Trainee Diary Entries – Day 1

Anxious Annie: Day 1

Phew! I'm exhausted. There's so much to take in! We started off with a fairly relaxed "getting to know you" session, where all the trainees, as we're called, did some activities that we could use in class with our students. There are some really good activities, and the other trainees all seem really nice. I worked with Fastidious Felicity for a while, she seems really friendly, if not a little scary to someone like me. She studied to be a high school teacher, so is quite confident in the classroom, and doesn't feel at all daunted by the idea of standing up in front of a class.

Next up was a lesson in Arabic!! The idea was that we get to feel what it's like to be a student in a language classroom. This was great fun, although I was rubbish at the pronunciation, I just couldn't get my mouth round some of the sounds they have. I thought it'd be awful to have the other students laughing at my pronunciation, but, because the tutor had created a relaxed atmosphere in the classroom, and we were all in the same boat, I didn't mind as much as I'd thought. At times, we all got a bit lost which must be how students feel in an English lesson, too, so it was a really useful experience- I'll also know how to say "I like swimming" in Arabic, if I'm ever in that part of the world!

I'm really glad I spent the weekend preparing for the course. There was an awful lot of administrative work to take care of, and I don't think my brain would have coped, if I hadn't thought about things before we started.

I've now got to think about my instructions for tomorrow - our first lesson with real students! I'm sooooo nervous already. I just hope I don't dry up when I get up in front of the class. Our group spent some time talking through tomorrow's lesson with our TP tutor - luckily we don't have to write a plan for the first lesson - I think that would've finished me off! I'm up after Harassed Henry so I'm hoping he'll have broken the ice with the students. Glad I'm not first - that would've been even worse!!

Although I'm really anxious about our first lesson, I'm also quite excited about meeting the students, and seeing what it really feels like to be up at the front there. I think our TP group will work well together and we'll all bring certain things to the class. Chilled-out Charlie's really laid-back so that'll compensate for my nerves and maybe I can get some tips from him and Fastidious Felicity on how to be more confident in front of the class.

Chilled-out Charlie (CC) **has decided not to keep a diary, but has allowed us to listen in on his conversations with his flat-mate, Laid-back Larry (LL).**

LL: Alright, mate? How was your day? Fancy a beer?

CC: Man, I need one! I get what they meant, when they kept banging on about the course being intensive during the interviews. What a day! I really should've spent the weekend getting myself sorted.

LL: What do you mean? I thought you said it'd be a breeze.

CC: I might've underestimated it. I didn't get off to the best of starts. Rolled up dead on 9am, but everyone else was already there and the tutor was looking at his watch, waiting for me, so he could get started. He didn't say anything, but I could tell he wasn't impressed. I'm gonna have to try and get up 15 minutes earlier tomorrow. Damn that snooze button!

LL: Well, just make sure you don't wake me up! What are the other people on the course like?

CC: They all seem ok; I sat with a guy named Harassed Henry, who arrived just before me. Fastidious Felicity, another trainee, is ultra-organised, so she can tell me what to do and when!

LL: She sounds awful!

CC: I think she means well! She helped me out a lot today, there's so much we have to remember.

LL: Sounds like a right pain. I thought you were just gonna learn how to teach?

CC: Yep, we get stuck in with the students tomorrow! We were told exactly what we'll be teaching, which is great as it means I don't need to do much preparation tonight, I'll just read through the notes. It'll be good to get into the classroom, I'm sure it won't feel much different from my other classes, and, as I'm starting with the intermediate class, I can have a bit of a laugh and a joke with them, that'll soon fill up the time.

LL: Yeah, you'll have them eating out of your hand in no time!

CC: Right, I must finish that pre-course task- it's actually really useful stuff. I don't know why I didn't do it a while ago. I do really want to do well on this course!

Harassed Henry: Day 1

Cor blimey, I never knew you could do so much in one day. I got to the school at about ten to nine, so plenty of time for a 9am start, and therefore decided to get a coffee. As it turns out, I should've just gone straight to the room, because I actually couldn't find it. I got really panicky, until I spotted Anxious Annie, who I'd met on the day of the interview. I followed her, and eventually walked into the room at one minute to nine. I wasn't the last person though, that was Chilled-out Charlie, he looked so embarrassed when the tutor just stared at him! I don't think he was really angry, but probably just trying to make a point. He later told us how important it'll be to make sure we are on time for everything throughout the course. I definitely don't want to get in his bad books so I'll never be late for anything!

So, first up we learned about how we can break the ice with the learners who we'll be meeting and teaching tomorrow - aaaagh! The tutor had some great "getting to know you" activities. We tried a few out on each other - by the end of the session, I felt that I knew everything there is to know about Anxious Annie, Chilled-out Charlie and Fastidious Felicity. They're all really nice, so I'm looking forward to teaching with them tomorrow. Fastidious Felicity helped me a lot in the admin session. The tutor told us that we have to keep our portfolio up to date, but filing really isn't my strong point - I'll just follow everything Fastidious Felicity does - I can't go wrong then!

We were given our lesson plan for the first lesson with the students. The tutor explained what we have to do, but I'm not really sure I understood her. I'll have to have a look through the plan again, once the kids have gone to bed.

I hated the Arabic session, I felt like a right plonker, because I couldn't pronounce the words correctly, and the teacher got me to repeat it again, and again, and again. Luckily she didn't just pick on me; sometimes we "drilled" all together. I'll have to remember that feeling when I'm the teacher.

Right, best get the kids to bed then make sure I know what I'm doing tomorrow. One of the tutors suggested keeping a diary of our experiences throughout the course. I'm actually quite enjoying writing this, so I'll try to keep it up. It'll be really interesting to read it at the end of the course, to see how I've progressed (if at all!).
Uh oh, Pleasant Pat is calling me to make sure the kids have cleaned their teeth. I might have to have a word with her this evening about how stressful this course is going to be, and how much time I have to spend in the evenings getting ready for the next day - I'm sure she'll understand.

Fastidious Felicity: Day 1

I am so glad that I'm me! Thank goodness I spent the weekend getting organised, and I'm really pleased that I went to the school last Friday to see where the classroom is - the building is a maze and the room numbering really is very silly.

I've had a great day. We were given lots of information about the course, and what we've got to do to keep our portfolio in order. Harassed Henry kept asking me questions about what the tutor had told us in the admin session. He seems like he's really disorganised, so I can see I'll have to take him under my wing and make sure he keeps his portfolio up-to-date!

Our first session was fun, we all just got to know each other, and then we had a foreign language lesson. We were taught a little bit of Arabic. It was weird, not being able to understand anything the teacher was saying, it's really important that I remember this when I start teaching.

We were given a lesson plan to teach from tomorrow. I wish they'd let us write our own lesson plan, I'm not really convinced that my part of the lesson is the best way to do it, I would've done it differently. I guess I just have to trust that the tutors know what they're doing until I find my feet.

I'm now going to organise my bag for tomorrow, and file all the handouts we were given today, I think I'll create another file just for input sessions. It looks like this course is going to produce quite a lot of paper.

Organising Your Time

Every Evening during the Course

Fastidious Felicity uses her bus journey home from the school to make a list of the jobs she needs to do before she goes to bed. When she gets home, she gives herself an hour to have some dinner and relax. She then sits down to do the jobs on her evening to-do list. She'll be up till late working on her lesson plan, but, because she filled her sleep bank at the weekend, she knows that she can handle it.

Harassed Henry falls asleep on the train home so doesn't have a chance to write his to-do list. When he gets home, Pleasant Pat and the children are waiting for him to have dinner with them. He's pleased to see the family, and is glad that dinner is on the table. After dinner, Harassed Henry tries to tell the children that "Daddy has to go and do some work", but of course they stick out their bottom lips and Daddy crumbles and has a quick game on the games console with them. Henry finally sits down to write his lesson plan at 9pm, when the kids have gone to bed. Unfortunately, because he didn't utilise his journey home to write an evening to-do list, he forgets that he also has to write a self-evaluation. He wakes up at 4am, after a couple of hours of sleep, suddenly remembering the self-evaluation.

Every Weekend during the Course

Fastidious Felicity, Chilled-out Charlie, Harassed Henry and Anxious Annie all go to the pub on Friday evening. They all kick back and relax with a few beers. They have a great night together, and find that, although they're all completely different, they do have at least two things in common, a love of English and a love of beer! Harassed Henry and Anxious Annie leave after a couple, but Chilled-out Charlie and Fastidious Felicity decide to make more of a night of it, as they seem to be hitting it off.

Fastidious Felicity wakes up late on Saturday morning, and decides to have a nice brunch with her boyfriend, Jolly John, before writing a weekend to-do list. By writing the list now, she knows exactly what she needs to have done by the time she goes to bed on Sunday evening. She plans her weekend around the tasks she has to complete. She decides to get most of the work done on Saturday afternoon/evening, so that she can have a full day off on Sunday. She completes her written assignment, and then writes a lesson plan. She needs to focus on the target language and ends up analysing all the aspects mentioned in her grammar book, just to ensure that she's being thorough enough.

Chilled-out Charlie also has a lie-in on Saturday morning and unfortunately he decides not to think about CELTA at all today, instead he'll leave it till Sunday. Chilled-out Charlie is talked into going to a party on Saturday evening, so he doesn't get to bed until late. When he finally wakes up on Sunday, at noon, he decides to jot down a list to see what he has to do. It becomes clear that there's quite a lot to do before he can go to bed on Sunday evening - not good with a hangover. It looks as if it's going to be another late night.

Needless to say, Fastidious Felicity's going to start another intensive week on a better foot than Chilled-Out Charlie. Let's just hope that Harassed Henry and Anxious Annie have followed Fastidious Felicity's good example, but without having done the superfluous language analysis, which will only end up causing her confusion later on.

Being Prepared

Chilled-out Charlie sets his alarm for 8.15 am. After all, 45 minutes to get up, shower, have breakfast, pack his bag and get to school should surely be plenty of time. Unfortunately, Charlie arrives at the platform just as the train's pulling away. When he does finally arrive at school, he has to queue while the 3 teachers in front of him make copies for their 9am classes. He dashes into lesson planning at 9.03, a disorganised pile of papers spilling out of his folder, and has to spend the next three minutes sorting out what needs to be handed in, and what's for him to keep.

Fastidious Felicity's at an advantage in this part of the course. Every evening, she checks her timetable to see what she might need the following day, such as her record booklet (CELTA 5), coursebook, observation tasks or a self-evaluation form, and puts them in her bag. She looks to see what time she needs to be at school, and thinks about whether she needs to do any photocopying before the course starts in the morning. Sounds sickeningly organised? That may be, but her tutors will appreciate her preparation skills and she's certainly making her own life a lot easier.

Now that the course has started, you are going to have to really work hard at organising your time and using every last minute to full effect. Try to plan ahead, so that you know what you need to do, and when you need to do it. If you tend to be disorganised, this doesn't mean you can't succeed on the course but it does mean you may need to make a little more effort with the administrative side. Use any spare moments you may have to make sure you have done everything you need to do, a to-do list may prove very helpful. In the long run, Chilled-out Charlie would help himself if he could be a little more like Fastidious Felicity in his daily preparation.

Tips for Organising Time

- Make sure you're always aware of deadlines for written assignments.

- Don't do more than required. You might think you are covering all bases by analysing all uses of "will", but, by not being able to focus only on the target language you are, in fact, demonstrating a lack of language awareness.

- Try not to leave anything till the last minute.

- Things like photocopying often take longer than you think - be prepared for this.

- Try to keep your filing up-to-date - it takes less time if you do it day by day, rather than leaving it all to the day before your portfolio needs to be handed in. It also means that you're less likely to lose anything and it's a good way to review what you have learned at the end of each day.

- Trawling the internet for a particular activity can be very time-consuming; it's usually quicker just to design your own.

- If you're not teaching the following day, make the most of the evening and get on with a written assignment or your next lesson plan if you can.

- Think about keeping a diary during the course. This could prove useful when it comes to writing written assignments and when evaluating your own teaching.

Input Sessions

Case Study 1 - Classroom Management

Anxious Annie and Fastidious Felicity are sitting together for the input session. The topic is classroom management, a really interesting topic for Anxious Annie, as she's been struggling to get the class's attention after an activity, so she hopes she'll find out how to do this during the session.

Chilled-out Charlie and Harassed Henry are also sitting together. Chilled-out Charlie's already been praised for his classroom management by his tutors, so he relaxes in this session, whereas Harassed Henry isn't sure what classroom management entails, so is determined to listen carefully, and take in as much as possible.

The tutor hands out a worksheet for the trainees to work through in pairs. Fastidious Felicity and Anxious Annie work through the worksheet together, discussing the questions and possible answers in detail. At the same time Chilled-out Charlie is completing the worksheet, without really discussing it with Harassed Henry, hoping he can get through it as quickly as possible. "Don't worry Henry, I know all the answers, we've got this one in the bag." Chilled-out Charlie feels that this input session's a bit of a waste of time really.

By working well together, and generating a lot of discussion, both Fastidious Felicity and Anxious Annie will have learned something during this task. They may not have got all the answers correct, but, at least they've discussed it and have considered all aspects. While Chilled-out Charlie and Harassed Henry did indeed get all the answers correct, Harassed Henry is none the wiser, and will continue to struggle with classroom management when teaching.

The tutor conducts feedback with the whole class after this task, and, as Anxious Annie and Fastidious Felicity are still discussing question 6, she asks Anxious Annie how she'd get the class's attention after group or pair work - Anxious Annie realises that by directing the question at her, the tutor has demonstrated one way of getting a student's attention if they are not listening, so suggests that this would be a good way. The tutor is pleased that Anxious Annie has realised that the input sessions are also valuable for getting ideas for their own classroom teaching.

Harassed Henry still hasn't got a clue, he's not at all sure what classroom management really is. As he and his partner have got all the answers right in the task, he doesn't feel comfortable asking the tutor to explain in more detail. He'll talk to Anxious Annie about it later, if he can find the time.

Harassed Henry's now increased his workload even more, and will possibly take some precious time away from Anxious Annie.

Harassed Henry: Day 3

Oh God, I taught an awful lesson today. My tutor commented on the fact that, throughout the lesson, I was blocking Susanne, who was sitting at the end of the horseshoe. Apparently, she couldn't see the board at all, I really should've noticed this, and moved her to sit with the others at the beginning. Not only that, but according to my peers in feedback, I was talking louder and louder, to try to get the students to listen to me when I wanted to move on from the speaking activity - Chilled-out Charlie said I should've got them to stop talking before I started. In feedback, Fastidious Felicity pointed out that both these points came up in the classroom management input session. I'm so annoyed with Chilled-out Charlie for not taking that session more seriously - just because he's good at it, doesn't mean we all are. I cornered Anxious Annie after feedback and asked to borrow her classroom management notes, so I can be sure not to make such basic mistakes next time.

Let's hope Pleasant Pat's got the lasagne in the oven, after the day I've had, I need a bit comfort food.

Case Study 2 - Reading Skills

Chilled-out Charlie thinks this session might be quite useful. He has a bit of teaching experience, and, although he mostly just chats in his lessons, he's tried using some newspaper articles. When he does a reading text in any of his classes, he usually asks the students to read the text out loud, and then underline all the words they don't know, which they then discuss. He's interested to see if these are the techniques the tutor talks about as well.

Chilled-out Charlie's amazed to find out that there are so many activities you can do with a reading text, other than just doing comprehension questions, and discussing it. It dawns on him that he's the one who ends up doing most of the talking in the discussion based on the text, because the students haven't really got to grips with the text first. Now he thinks about it, it is difficult to understand a text while reading out loud, and the tutor's right, when she says that the students don't need to understand every word. He's really looking forward to his next reading skills lesson in TP, and hopes he'll be able to try out the sub-skills that they've learnt about in this input session.

Fastidious Felicity knows lots of the techniques the tutor's talking about from her Italian lessons. Her Italian teacher is very good, and does lots of interesting things with reading texts, however, Felicity really struggles with guessing unknown words from the context, she'd much rather just look them up in her English-Italian dictionary.

By the end of the input session, Fastidious Felicity has resolved to not take her bilingual dictionary to her next Italian lesson. She can see now why it's so important to guess words from context, and feels she'll also be able to use her own learning experience in helping her students. She's also looking forward to teaching a reading lesson, now they've had an input session on it.

Chilled-out Charlie: Day 7

CC: Hey, Larry! Crack open a beer, we've got to celebrate.

LL: What're we celebrating, mate?

CC: I just taught my best lesson yet - got a TS+ for it!

LL: What's a TS+?

CC: Above standard! It was great! I taught a reading skills lesson, and brought in loads of aspects we spoke about in the reading skills input session the other day.

LL: That's great! Well done.

CC: Yeah, I'm well chuffed. My tutor said my plan still wasn't detailed enough, but I can work on that. At least the lesson itself went like a dream - I know I'm gonna be a great teacher!

LL: What did the others think about your lesson?

CC: Everyone was really positive about my lesson, and I got loads of praise. Anxious Annie noticed that I even got my instructions in before giving out the handout. Poor Fastidious Felicity hasn't managed to get a

TS+ yet, I'm sure she thinks she should've been the first to get one.

LL: Can you have a night off tonight, then?

CC: Nah, 'fraid not. I need to crack on with my next plan while I'm feeling inspired, but a swift one to get me started won't harm!

Case Study 3 - Error Correction

Anxious Annie sits down next to Harassed Henry. He always seems to be quite good at error correction, and Anxious Annie worries about showing students up in front of the others when she tries. When Fastidious Felicity tried to do error correction in class, she seemed to really put the students on the spot. Anxious Annie would hate to be picked on, so that must be how some students feel as well. This is an input session she really wants to get to grips with, as it's often mentioned in the "points to work on" part of her feedback.

After working through a handout, which she discusses with Harassed Henry, Anxious Annie realises that doing error correction in class doesn't have to involve showing students up in front of the others. They discuss how there are two different kinds of error correction, the second of which Anxious Annie's never really thought about. Next, they have a handout with different activities on, and they have to decide what kind of error correction they would do for each activity. Harassed Henry points out a basic rule of thumb that really helps Anxious Annie - if it's a fluency activity, do error correction after the activity. If it's an activity for accuracy, then error correction should be immediate.

Anxious Annie asks the tutor how immediate error correction can be done sensitively, so the tutor demonstrates some techniques, such as peer-correction, self-correction and finger-correction, all of which Anxious

Annie admits she would feel quite comfortable with, if she were the student or the teacher.

By the end of the session Anxious Annie feels a lot more comfortable about the idea of correcting students' errors, and she resolves to try out some in her next lesson.

Anxious Annie: Day 9

Well that didn't go quite as well as I'd hoped it might, but, at least, my tutor noticed my attempt at incorporating error correction. I taught lexis and speaking today. I introduced students to lexis used to talk about things in the home, and then gave them a freer practice activity, where they had to describe their own homes to their partner. As discussed in the error correction input session, I listened carefully, and made a note of errors the students made with the target language. I found it really hard to concentrate and actually hear the mistakes, but I did manage to pick up a couple of things. I put the errors on the board in post-fluency feedback, and asked the students if they could correct them. On one occasion, the student who'd made the mistake actually said "oh that was me" - initially I felt terrible that he'd realised I was using his error but he seemed really pleased, and was able to correct it himself. I guess I've got to stop worrying about making people feel silly, they're there to learn after all.

So, now my point to work on is checking students' understanding of new lexis. I shouldn't assume that just because one person's shown that they understand something, the whole class understands. I need to get the hang of using these awful concept checking questions......

Use input sessions to learn as much as possible, if you are asked to discuss in pairs, do just that. It's not about who finishes the activity first, it's about who gains the most from the discussion.

Input sessions are tutor-led lessons. They are usually inductive and hands-on, and trainees are very involved. The input sessions relate to the actual teaching, so a good trainee will be able to put newly introduced methods into practice in their teaching.

Checklist

☑ Have you filed your notes and handouts from input sessions, so they are easy to refer to?

Lesson Planning

The tutor hands out the notes for the next lesson, and asks Fastidious Felicity, Chilled-out Charlie, Anxious Annie and Harassed Henry to read through what they, and their planning partners, are going to be teaching in tomorrow's lesson. Fastidious Felicity reads through the notes carefully, and then reads through Harassed Henry's notes. Harassed Henry's still trying to cut up 26 bits of paper that he needs for today's lesson, as he didn't have time to do it last night. Chilled-out Charlie doesn't really read through the notes very carefully, but thinks he knows what he's got to do, so starts to talk to Anxious Annie about her journey to school that morning. Anxious Annie points out that, as they don't have a huge amount of time, maybe they should get on with the planning.

Once they've all settled down, they only actually have 30 minutes left with their tutor. Fastidious Felicity's written her aims, and has a list of questions she wants to check with the tutor. She makes notes as the tutor answers her questions, so she'll remember everything when she sits down to write her lesson plan in the evening.

Chilled-out Charlie's got completely the wrong end of the stick, as he didn't read through his TP points properly, so his time with the tutor's taken up with trying to work out what he's going to be teaching. He thinks he'll remember everything his tutor says, so doesn't bother writing anything down.

Writing the actual plan

Fastidious Felicity sits down in the evening to write her plan. She's teaching a lesson on "will" for spontaneous decisions, but decides to analyse all aspects of the "will future" just to be on the safe side.

Chilled-out Charlie knows what he'll say to the class when telling them how to play the hot seat game, so doesn't include these instructions on his plan.

Harassed Henry has to get dinner for the kids, as his wife has gone out for her Spanish evening class. Again, it's after 9pm before he can sit down and start on his lesson plan. It's going to be another night with little sleep for him.

Fastidious Felicity: Day 9

I hate Gracious Gertrude; she's not very gracious at all! She was really rude today in my grammar lesson. I was teaching "will" for spontaneous decisions, and she kept asking me why we don't say "I close the window", instead of "I'll close the window". I didn't know how to answer this question - I'd analysed all uses of "will", but didn't expect anyone to ask such a stupid question. My tutor pointed out that I might've anticipated this as a problem, if I'd only focused in depth on just the target language in my language analysis. Now I realise she's right, but I'm so annoyed, because I spent so much time on my language analysis, only for my lesson plan to be graded "to standard". I'll never get that 'A' grade, if I don't start getting "above standard" in lessons and for my plans. Chilled-out Charlie got an above standard grade for his lesson today, I'm sure I can do better than him! Grrrrrr!

Chilled-out Charlie: Day 10

LL: How was your day, pal?

CC: Not too bad. I think I'm finally getting to grips with writing lesson plans. I never seemed to have enough detail in mine for the tutor's liking.

LL: How detailed do they have to be?

CC: My tutor told me that I should write it so that someone else could teach from it. I tried imagining Harassed Henry trying to teach from my plan, so I even scripted the instructions I'd give to the students. It worked for me anyway. I don't always follow the instructions I've written down, but the fact that I've thought about them beforehand helps me keep my waffle down to a minimum.

LL: Sounds like a lot of work to me.

CC: It is, but I reckon it might be worth it. Writing a good lesson plan's been the most difficult part of the course for me, it just doesn't come naturally to have every tiny detail scripted. Fastidious Felicity seems to work better that way, but it's taken me a while to find the method that suits me best. I think I'm finally there now.

LL: Well, each to their own. I don't think I could be bothered to spend more time writing the plan than teaching the lesson.

CC: Yeah, but it'll get easier and, therefore, quicker I hope, and of course lesson plans can be re-used with other classes, too. At the beginning of this course, I couldn't wait for it to finish, so I could stop spending hours on planning and go back to my normal ad-lib style. I know I'm not gonna have this much time to spend on each plan when I'm back out there teaching 25 hours a week, but I'm definitely gonna stick to the basic structure that we've learnt.

LL: How did Fastidious Felicity do today?

CC: Oh, poor thing. I felt so sorry for her today. Up until now the tutors have always been positive about her lessons but today she had a really bad one.

LL: Why, what happened?

CC: We've all had a tough week, but she's felt it more than others. I don't think she's had as much time to spend on each plan, and it was really noticeable today. She came really unstuck when the students didn't get involved in an activity the way she'd expected them to. Then she kept repeating her instructions. With each instruction she was talking more and more, and then she kept interrupting them to explain again. We were all sat at the back cringing, and feeling really sorry for her. She was in tears in feedback, but we managed to give her a boost, the tutor really focused on the positive points in her lesson.

LL: Oh, poor her, I never thought I'd find myself feeling sorry for her, but it sounds like she's really putting herself under pressure. Am I going to get to meet her? I'm sure I could focus on her positive points!

CC: Yeah, she certainly doesn't make life easy for herself. Now, shall we go out for a beer - it is Friday after all!

Anxious Annie: Day 11

I had to leave the class after my lesson today, as I was almost in tears, I just can't seem to get a grip on my nerves. In feedback, all the other trainees were really supportive, and gave me a boost, as did the tutor. She told me to persevere and that things will fall into place soon. She told me that I design such lovely materials and activities, which is something that I really enjoy doing. She also said my lesson plans are really thorough, so all the work I put in on them is, at least, paying off, I just wish I could put them to good use in the classroom, instead of panicking. Everyone said I don't come across as nervous as I did at the beginning of the course, but I still feel it.

Before the lesson started, Fastidious Felicity offered to be my guinea pig, which was really nice of her. Of course, everything went smoothly when I ran through the lesson with her, as there was no-one watching, and I didn't feel like she was judging me, but it's just when I stand up in front of the class that I go to pieces.

For each lesson that you teach, you have a planning session with your tutor. At the beginning of the course, the notes you are given are detailed and structured, and you are given a lot of support in your teaching. As the course progresses, the notes become sparser, and you can become more independent in what you teach. You are, however, never left completely to your own devices. In the planning session, you have the chance to ask your tutor any questions about your lesson, and it's a good idea at this stage to make copious notes that'll help you in the evening, when you come to write your lesson plan. The planning session is also an opportunity to work with your peers. Other trainees can often give you good ideas for your lessons, so you don't need to feel you're on your own when it comes to planning.

To start with, it will take you a long time to write lesson plans, so be prepared for this. Your plan needs to contain the aims of the lesson, the materials you are going to use, an analysis of the language you are going to introduce, and a detailed procedure of what you and the students are going to do in class.

Fastidious Felicity spent far too much time analysing "will" and gave herself extra unnecessary work. Chilled-out Charlie came unstuck in class when giving his instructions. As he didn't write them down on his plan, he waffled on, explaining the same thing five times to confused-looking students and then didn't understand why he ran out of time during the game he was doing. Harassed Henry was exhausted after his late night, but did a good job in class. He's not making things easy for himself though. By not having completely cleared his diary for the duration of the course he is not really reaching his full potential.

Checklist

☑ Do my aims correspond with the focus of my lesson (for example reading or grammar)?

☑ Have I completed all the sections on the lesson plan?

☑ If I have copied and pasted from another plan, or an earlier section of my plan, is it still appropriate?

☑ Have I included my materials with my plan?

☑ Is my procedure detailed enough, so that another teacher could teach from it?

☑ Have I incorporated into my plan what we have looked at during input sessions?

☑ Is my language analysis thorough enough, but relevant only to the aspects I'm really introducing in my lesson?

☑ Are my teaching development aims realistic?

☑ Have I written the latest lesson plan with the tutors' comments on previous plans in mind?

Teaching Practice

Harassed Henry's standing in front of the students who are chatting quietly amongst themselves. He has 3 minutes until he's due to start his first longer lesson, up until now he's just been teaching shorter slots. On the one hand he's a little anxious about filling the time, on the other he's relieved, as he thinks it might mean he won't have so many problems with timing, it won't matter if he goes slightly over on a fluency activity and the students just want to carry on talking. Lesson plan in hand, with his instructions highlighted, he welcomes the students, and gets started on his warmer. While the students are busy with this, he takes a look at his plan to see what is coming next and checks he has the materials ready to hand out. His lesson goes quite smoothly, although, he's still struggling with getting the students to stop talking at the end of an activity.

Fastidious Felicity's up next. She's prepared some lovely materials and flipchart pictures to make the lexis clear and is hoping the students will do the activity exactly as she's planned it. Unfortunately, the lesson will prove to be exhausting. She's got so many materials and spends most of the time rushing around, giving herself very little thinking time, resulting in her not being able to review her plan as much as she would like, and she ends up talking far too much. In freer practice, she keeps having to stop the students to give them extra instructions, because they aren't doing the activity exactly as she wants it. She tells them they should only talk about one question but they keep going on to the next one - very frustrating!

Chilled-out Charlie gives a lovely reading lesson and his tutor is really pleased. He's followed the stages they were introduced to in the reading input session, and remembers to give the students quiet time to read, rather than talking all the way through the students' reading time, like Harassed Henry had done the previous week. The activity that Fastidious Felicity helped him with in lesson planning works really well, and he even manages to keep his TTT (teacher talking time) to a minimum, remembering that his role isn't that of an entertainer in the classroom. He doesn't even feel that his rapport suffers, and he still manages to have a joke with Joyful Giovanni at the end. Unfortunately his peer observation is not as successful as his lesson.

Harassed Henry: Day 12

I'm fuming! Had a go at Chilled-out Charlie today. I don't often lose my rag but he was really out of order. He sat through the whole of TP doing nothing but planning tomorrow's lesson just so he could watch the footie tonight. Then when it came to giving feedback, inevitably, he had nothing to say. The rest of the group tries really hard to give useful feedback to support each other and he gets away with not paying attention just 'cos he manages to talk his way out of things. I suppose I shouldn't have had such a go but I'm feeling the pressure this week as it is, and his behaviour just tipped me over the edge. He did realise that he was out of order, and I could tell all the others agreed with me. It's just not fair. I stayed behind after feedback to talk everything through with the tutor. She said she'd have a quiet word with Chilled-out Charlie tomorrow but she was fairly sure that me having a go at him would've shaken him up and made him realise that he's slacking. My actual lesson went better than anticipated. I didn't really know what to expect with the longer lesson. I was a bit worried that I wouldn't be able to fill the time, but it turns out that as long as you've planned well, you really can keep students occupied and possibly even learning for quite a while! I realised today how helpful a well-organised plan can be. I decided to follow Fastidious Felicity's suggestion of highlighting my instructions in the lesson plan, so that I can see them easily, it really helped. The only thing that went wrong was not being able to get the students' attention after the fluency task. I don't like raising my voice, or banging on tables, so I need to find something that will work for me. I'm sure there was something else that was mentioned in the classroom management session, so I'll check with the notes that Anxious Annie lent me. My tutor told me off for having an untidy whiteboard, but I'm

 not too worried about that, I know I can improve my handwriting on the board fairly

easily. Right am off to take the dog for a walk- that always calms me down!

Fastidious Felicity: Day 12

Phew, that was exhausting! I was really well organised and spent ages preparing all my materials and then it still fell flat. It was slightly annoying that I'd spent so long on my plan, but then didn't have time to look at it at all during the lesson, good job I'd read it through several times before the lesson started. I'd prepared some beautiful drawings on flipchart paper to put up on the board, which showed the adjectives I was introducing, but my magnets kept sliding down, so, instead of concentrating on giving my concept questions, I had to keep putting them back in place. Also, these students just don't seem to do what I want them to. The other trainees suggested I should be a little less controlling, but I'm sure that'll just mean the students listen to my instructions even less than they do now!

I hate to admit it, but I'm a bit envious of Chilled-out Charlie, he seems to be able to charm all the students, even Gracious Gertrude. He's so relaxed about it all, and still does really well. I'm sure I have the ability to be as good in the classroom as he is, after all, the activity that he used today was something that the two of us came up with together in planning.

Chilled-out Charlie and Harassed Henry got into a bit of a fight today during feedback. Harassed Henry had a right go at Chilled-out Charlie for not taking much notice of other people's lessons. Today, as soon as he'd finished his lesson, Chilled-out Charlie sat down and started working on his next lesson plan. He wasn't able to give any of us decent feedback. I think our tutor was annoyed and would have said something but Harassed Henry got in there first, he was so angry!

> There are a lot of things to think about in TP, but you should remember that most of these things will become second nature over time, and you won't have to think about them all the time. Your lesson plan is there to help you, make sure you will be able to follow it even when there is a lot going on during the lesson; after all, you spent all that time writing it. Try and integrate what you cover in input sessions, and you will find yourself meeting the criteria.

Checklist

☑ Have I organised all my materials so they are ready to hand out?

☑ Have I done what I can before the lesson starts to ensure it runs smoothly?

☑ Do I know what time my lesson starts and finishes?

☑ Do I know which of my peers I am handing over to?

☑ Can I see a clock?

☑ Is the CD player working, and ready to go?

☑ Have I checked that the projector/interactive whiteboard are fully functional?

☑ Do the board pens work?

☑ Have I got my lesson aims in mind?

☑ Can I remember the students' names? If not, have I got name cards for them?

Feedback

Fastidious Felicity, Harassed Henry and Chilled-out Charlie have taught, Anxious Annie had a "day off".

The tutor asks everyone, teaching and non-teaching trainees, to think about the lessons they taught, or observed, and write down three positives and three areas which need improvement onto the whiteboard for discussion later.

Fastidious Felicity's first in with three positives about her own lesson and several about both Harassed Henry's and Chilled-out Charlie's lessons too. Harassed Henry's pleased with the way his lesson went, so bites the bullet, and writes down 2 positives for his lesson, he only hopes his tutor saw it the same way. He doesn't struggle to find negative points, he knows he still needs to improve, especially keeping his whiteboard tidy. Anxious Annie writes down a positive point for all three teachers' lessons, but she doesn't feel she's in a position to point out any negatives; she'll leave that to the tutor. Chilled-out Charlie writes some good things down about his own lesson but is struggling to think of anything to say about the other lessons he supposedly observed, because he had been planning his next lesson instead of concentrating on theirs, so he writes "TTT" in the negative section and "good whiteboard use" in the positive section, knowing that the tutor's bound to talk about these points, because she always does. He adds to the positive column that both the other lessons were really good.

The tutor tries to encourage Fastidious Felicity to think of some points to work on for her lesson. When she can't come up with anything, the tutor asks if she thinks her lesson was perfect, Fastidious Felicity admits that it wasn't, and quickly adds a couple more negative points.

Harassed Henry's asked to expand on the positive points that he wrote down, and the other trainees are asked whether they agree with him - they do. The tutor then confirms that, indeed, he should be pleased with today's lesson; he's clearly worked hard on the areas he was asked to. Harassed Henry wrote down a few negatives and he's asked to discuss why he thinks he is struggling to keep his whiteboard tidy, he comes up with some good suggestions of what he might be doing wrong. Again, the tutor agrees. Harassed Henry's proving to be very good at evaluating his own lessons and a useful member in feedback sessions.

Anxious Annie's asked to explain the positive points she noted down, the tutor disagrees slightly with one of her points. After a short discussion, and an explanation from the tutor, all trainees can see why she doesn't agree that it should be on the positive side. Anxious Annie's pleased that she wrote this down, it was an area she thought she was doing badly in, because her peers did it differently to her, the tutor has now indirectly confirmed that she should stick to her method. Anxious Annie vows to muster up the confidence to contribute more in feedback sessions in future.

Chilled-out Charlie is asked why he's written "TTT" in the negative section. He says that he thinks there was generally too much TTT during the lessons, but, when pushed to give examples, he can't come up with any. The other trainees are asked whether they agree with Chilled-out Charlie's evaluation of TTT. They all disagree, as does the tutor.

Chilled-out Charlie: Day 12

LL: All right, mate? How was your day?

CC: It was OK until our feedback session this evening. Harassed Henry really lost it with me tonight.

LL: Why? What happened?

CC: Well, to cut a long story short, I got a bit caught out in feedback. The tutor expects us to have a lot to say, but as soon as I finished teaching I just switched off so hadn't really been paying much attention. I said that I thought all the lessons were good, but, when pressed for more, I came a bit unstuck. I didn't know what to say, so I said that the TTT was a bit high.

LL: TTT?

CC: The amount the teacher talks in class. Anyway, I could tell she wasn't pleased with my contribution, and, as it turns out, they all agreed that the TTT was much *lower* today! Then Harassed Henry said he thought it was really out of order that I was sitting in TP and not concentrating on the lessons. He said that all the rest of the group paid attention so that they could give constructive feedback and I just sat there and tried to get ahead so I didn't have to do so much in the evening. I could tell the rest of the group, as well as the tutor, agreed with him and I felt awful. Even Anxious Annie was nodding her head when Harassed Henry was having a go!

LL: God! That sounds a bit heavy!

CC: Well he does have a point, I guess. I apologised to him afterwards and he said sorry for losing it. Said he'd been really feeling the pressure this week as he's teaching 3 times, has to resubmit a written assignment as well as write the next one. Anyway, the upshot is that I really need to make sure I pay more attention, because I know how useful it is to have detailed feedback on your lesson. Fastidious Felicity and Harassed Henry always give honest feedback whenever I'm teaching. Think I better apologise to the rest of the group tomorrow. Don't want them thinking I'm not taking the whole thing seriously!

LL: I suppose it's inevitable that people get a bit stressed with the amount of work you all have to do. What've you got to do now? Can't you watch the whole game with me? I've got some beer in the fridge.

CC: I've just got to write up my lesson plan. Let me crack on, and I'll be with you as soon as I can.

Anxious Annie: Day 13

YES!!! I did it! Finally a lesson where I managed to get on top of my nerves. The others were so pleased for me; it really felt like something just clicked. I managed to follow my plan, and had a great speaking activity that I'd designed myself and the students really enjoyed. The tutor said she noticed right from the start of the class that I seemed more relaxed. As I wasn't so nervous, it meant my instructions were very clear because I used them exactly as I had them on my plan, and didn't repeat them 6 times over.

I'm not teaching tomorrow, but am going to start working on my next plan now. I really feel like I did do well, and I hope my next few lessons go as smoothly. I know that a well-prepared lesson is key to giving me that extra bit of confidence I need. I'm teaching grammar next, prepositions of place, and I've got some great ideas of how to present and practise the language, using Cuisenaire rods so I'm looking forward to getting down to it.

By not seeing the positives in your own lessons, you are basically saying that you thought it was a fail lesson. In the same vein, if you cannot see the negatives, then you are suggesting there is no room for improvement. You must be able to evaluate your lessons realistically, don't be modest, but don't be conceited - just be honest. Giving feedback to your peers is equally as important, as you can all learn from each other. Of course, the tutor's feedback is invaluable, but there is no reason why you cannot see positive and negative aspects in each others' lessons as well, and learn from this. This can easily be done in a positive, sensitive way, without upsetting anyone, or causing offence. And remember, analysing mistakes affords us the opportunity to learn and so improve.

Self-evaluation

As soon as her lesson has finished, Anxious Annie sits down and writes her self-evaluation. She considers all aspects of the lesson, classroom management, the students and her teaching skills. She picks up on a lot of negative things about her lesson, but she doesn't want to focus on any positives. Who is she to say what was good about the lesson? That's up to the tutor.

The tutor reads Anxious Annie's self-evaluation, and gets a little annoyed. If Anxious Annie can't see anything good in her lesson, does that mean she can't see what a good lesson is?

Chilled-out Charlie finishes his lesson, but can't be bothered to write his self-evaluation, it's been a tough day. He knows he has to write one, because his tutor's nagged him every day about completing it, but he can't really see the point. Chilled-out Charlie fills in all the boxes of the self-evaluation by writing one sentence in each part.

The tutor looks at Chilled-out Charlie's self-evaluation, she makes a note on it that it's not detailed enough, but she doesn't write any more than that.

Harassed Henry completes his self-evaluation immediately after teaching, and, as he knows that he won't have any time to add to it when he gets home, he puts in a lot of detail. He focuses on both the positives and the negatives, he knows his lesson wasn't perfect, but he followed the tutor's advice from the previous feedback session, so is sure that he did a better job today than in his previous lesson.

The tutor's really pleased to read Harassed Henry's self-evaluation. He's thought a lot about the lesson, and knows where things didn't go quite as well as they might have done. At the same time, he can see where the lesson went well, and this was down to his positive reaction to tutor feedback. He really is working hard to improve his teaching.

Fastidious Felicity also completes her self-evaluation, but she only focuses on the positives, she thinks the lesson went well, and she's really pleased with it. The students seemed to really enjoy the lesson, and the negatives were really very minor, the sort of things that could happen in any lesson, so not even really worth mentioning.

The tutor agrees with Fastidious Felicity's evaluation of the things that went well, but she wishes she would also focus on the things she needs to work on. As Fastidious Felicity hasn't pointed out these minor things herself, the tutor now feels that she has to bring them up in feedback. Otherwise, how can the tutor be sure that Fastidious Felicity knows that she needs to continue working on these areas?

Fastidious Felicity: Day 13

The most important lesson I've learned this week is that, when I stop trying to be perfect at everything, I'm actually more confident in the classroom. I was always worrying about making sure my lesson plans were fantastic, so I ended up with 20-page lesson plans for 45 minute lessons. Whilst a detailed lesson plan is necessary, it still has to be concise enough to teach from. Over the past couple of TPs, I've limited the plan to a maximum of 10 pages, (including all language analysis), and now I find that it's much easier to actually handle in the lesson. Unfortunately, my tutor was not quite as pleased with my self-evaluation as I would have hoped, apparently I should highlight all the silly things that I did wrong otherwise the tutor won't know if I realise that they are areas I need to work on, I guess she can't read my mind so I should write it down. Anyway, nothing can spoil today; I had a wonderful moment with Gracious Gertrude this afternoon. Even though she's not in my class anymore, she came to me in the break to ask a grammar question.   She asked if she should say "I have been here **since** 5 years or **for** 5 years". Not only could I tell her which was right, but also why.   She walked away with a nice smile on her face.   I love Gracious Gertrude!

Harassed Henry: Day 14

Wow, what a fantastic day! I walked into the classroom 15 minutes early today, with all my photocopies and everything prepared for the day. I didn't even have to cut up little slips of paper, because I got the kids to do it for me last night - we had a great time catching up on the news from the day, whilst getting my lesson materials organised. Pleasant Pat was really happy, because it gave her time to do her Spanish homework.

We had an input session a few days ago about dealing with errors. It was really useful, and I was able to use some of the techniques we learned in my lesson this afternoon. I do find it difficult to spot errors, but I know it will get easier.

In my self evaluation I wrote about how I felt using these techniques and how I thought some had worked better than others. My tutor commented on this, she wrote that my error correction was generally good, but pointed out that I shouldn't have disturbed the students during a fluency activity to correct them. Of course, I should have known this, as we discussed it this morning.

In feedback Chilled-out Charlie picked me up on my instructions for one activity being too long, I agreed with him, and we worked out how I could've done it better. We're now well over halfway, I think I'm going to miss this course.

The self-evaluations will be useful at various times of the course. Firstly, by evaluating your lesson, you will become aware of what works well in the classroom, and what you need to work on. Secondly, these self-evaluations will be a valuable resource for completing one of your written assignments, which asks you to reflect on your own classroom teaching. The more detail you include in your self-evaluations, the easier you will find it to write this assignment. As well as focusing on things that have gone wrong in a lesson, your tutor will expect you to be able to discuss areas which worked well in the classroom.

Some centres will ask for your self-evaluations immediately after you teach, and some will want them to be handed in the following day. Whichever procedure you need to follow, you will find it quite hard to remember exactly what happened in your lesson, even just a few hours later, so your evaluation will tend to be more detailed if you do it straight after you finish teaching.

Checklist

☑ Have I focused on both the positives and the negatives of my lesson?

☑ Have I completed all sections with a suitable amount of detail?

Tutorials

Chilled-out Charlie is due for his tutorial at 11.50. He's just having a coffee before his slot when he sees Fastidious Felicity who was having her tutorial just before him. She reminds him that it's nearly his slot and that he should really be waiting outside the classroom. Chilled-out Charlie grabs his coffee and runs for it. When he gets to the classroom, his tutor is waiting for him with his CELTA 5 in front of her. They go through what he is doing well, and what he still needs to work on. The tutor brings up the incident with Harassed Henry and then asks him how *he thinks* the course is going. Chilled-out Charlie is embarrassed to find himself welling up. He can't believe it as he *never* cries. He finds himself apologising profusely. The tutor is very understanding and says it's all due to the course being so exhausting. She says Chilled-out Charlie should be very pleased with his progress and that he's on the way to getting an above standard grade. This cheers Chilled-out Charlie up hugely and he goes out of the tutorial feeling motivated and fired-up, ready for his next TP.

Chilled-out Charlie: Day 14

LL: So, what's the latest from the CELTA camp?
CC: Well, I had a tutorial today.
LL: What's that then?
CC: It's a chance to speak to your tutor alone.
LL: Ah right, so what did she say?
CC: Well, on the whole, I'm doing well. My points to work on included giving more useful

feedback which harks back to the problems I had the other day with Harassed Henry. I've also got to reflect more on my own lesson which basically means I need to write more on my self-evaluations after I've taught.

LL: And do they talk about what you're doing well too?

CC: Oh yeah, it was mostly really positive. I've really cut down on the TTT. My tutor said that as long as I continue to make progress and improve on the points she'd mentioned, then I could be in line for a grade higher than a pass, which is great!

LL: Oh, I thought it was just a case of passing or failing?

CC: No mate, you can get either a Pass, a Pass B or a Pass A, although apparently Pass A's are a bit like gold dust so I'm going to forget about that but a B would be quite cool. She said my lessons had become really student-centred and that I was very creative with my ideas. I'm writing much more detailed lesson plans now too.

LL: Great, well done! Sounds like we've got a reason to celebrate- shall we crack open a beer?

CC: Well just the one, I've got to plan a listening lesson for tomorrow and I want it to be a good one. I'm gonna aim for that B grade now.

On the course, you will be offered at least one opportunity to discuss your progress so far with your tutor. This is done individually, and you can also bring up any issues you may have. The tutor will discuss your strengths and weaknesses and what to work on in the next part of the course.

If you are in any danger of failing the course, you will be given a further tutorial and receive a letter, which outlines exactly what you need to do in order to pass the course. These are the things the tutors will be looking for in your remaining TPs.

Checklist

☑ Have I filled in the necessary sections of my CELTA 5 and handed it in on time?

☑ Have I made a note of any questions I want to ask my tutor?

Peer Observation

It's nearly 2 o'clock, and the students are gradually drifting into the classroom. Fastidious Felicity is teaching first, and is looking through her lesson plan one last time. Harassed Henry suddenly realises he doesn't know what the observation task for the day is, so asks Anxious Annie for a copy. He glances at it, and sees that he should have spoken to one of the other trainees about their lesson aims to be able to complete the task. He quickly goes over to Fastidious Felicity to ask her what her aims are, Fastidious Felicity isn't best pleased to be interrupted 2 minutes before her lesson.

Anxious Annie: Day 15

I really enjoyed watching the lessons today; it's amazing how much you notice when you've not got your own lesson to worry about! Fastidious Felicity was up first, she had, yet again, prepared so many materials that she wore me out just watching her, she was rushing from the flipchart to the board to the OHP, and, in the midst of all that, had millions of bits of coloured paper to hand out. It turned out that her bits of coloured paper had all got muddled, so there was a bit of confusion when it came to the matching exercise- I guess it just shows that even the most organised person can trip up, if they overdo it on the materials. By the time Fastidious Felicity sat down, she was quite red in the face and looked like she needed a large G&T to calm her down!

Harassed Henry was next and taught a good speaking lesson. In feedback, we talked about his classroom management, and I reminded him about those notes I gave him. He did ask the students to stop, but Mehmet and Svetla hadn't finished and so they wanted to carry on talking. Harassed Henry had this as a point to work on his feedback again, and the tutor said it's something he really should have got to grips with by now.

Chilled-out Charlie's listening skills lesson was really great. He has such a lovely manner with the students, and they really respond to him. Now he's getting to grips with his TTT, he seems to be doing really well. He also incorporated all the subskills of listening, that we learned about in the input session. The tutor was really pleased with his lesson, and he got another TS+ for it. I'd love to get one of those, but I'm just relieved to have finally got to grips with my nerves, so TS+ can wait!

Because I was just an observer today, I made lots of notes while watching the lessons, so, in feedback, I could contribute loads. I even managed to suggest to Fastidious Felicity that maybe "less is more" when it comes to materials; she took this quite well, and even agreed with me.

Fastidious Felicity: Day 16

Felt quite emotional in TP today, we've all come such a long way since day 1. After the disaster of my last lesson I am pleased to say that I have now, finally, had a lesson where I didn't over-prepare and could really exploit the materials I had. Anxious Annie's "less is more" comment yesterday was at the front of my mind when I was putting the lesson together. I got some great feedback from my tutor, and the others. Chilled-out Charlie thought everything seemed to fall into place, and noticed how the students really appreciated being given enough time to do things. I feel like it's really clicked that the students are adults, and need to be treated differently to high school kids. That's taken me a while to get. I finally got that TS+ that I've been hoping for throughout the course, but, after all that time waiting for it, I realised today that it doesn't really matter. It's not really about the grade, it's about preparing and teaching a lesson that the teacher and the students enjoy. It's about helping them to learn, and it's about doing it in an interesting way, and so the students feel like they're progressing.

Anxious Annie was very sweet in feedback; she said that we'd finally managed to learn from each other. She now has the confidence that she was missing, and I've developed the ability to consider the students' needs, which I didn't do before, and she's right. I've also learned to look more critically at myself, rather than always assuming my way is right, that's something that doesn't just affect my teaching, but a lot of aspects of my life - Jolly John will be pleased!

While your peers are teaching, you're expected to do peer observation tasks, to focus on either one area of their teaching or on the students. These tasks are invaluable. Some tasks are vital for completing written assignments, and others are used as the basis for discussion in feedback. Your tutor will not take kindly to you not having done them, after all, peer observation is one of the components of the course for several reasons:

- Observing lessons is part of the learning process - you can think about how you would do it if you were teaching that particular lesson.
- In feedback, you're expected to give, and receive, feedback from your peers. It's not only the tutors' job.
- You can use peer observation as the basis for written assignments.
- It is only fair to support your peers, by concentrating on their lesson when they are teaching.

Written Assignments

Chilled-out Charlie takes his coffee and cigarettes, and goes out for a break. He bumps into Fastidious Felicity in the corridor, and calls out to her, wanting to know what's up next. She's rushing past, as she wants to copy some materials from a resource book in the 15 minute break. "Written assignment support" she replies and then dashes off. "Hmm," thinks Chilled-out Charlie to himself, "that sounds like a breeze."

Anxious Annie makes copious notes during the WA support session, she's never very good at remembering what the tutors say when it comes to sitting down and writing her written assignments. She jots down the preferred format, highlights all the parts of the question that the tutor mentions, and, in the brainstorming session, she gets out her notes from the observation tasks, which she's sure will be useful. By the end of the session, she's quite confident that she'll crack this written assignment first go, and resolves to get on with it that evening, while it's all still fresh in her mind.

One week later ...

As the tutor sits down she pulls the first written assignment from the top of the pile, it's Chilled-out Charlie's. She sighs as she looks at it - he clearly wasn't listening when she suggested they use a table format, and as a result she has to re-read it several times. He's completely forgotten one section, he obviously didn't bother with the checklist once he'd finished. He'll have to resubmit this one.

Anxious Annie's written assignment is clearly set out. She's answered all parts of the question, and backed it up with classroom examples - a clear pass.

Anxious Annie: Day 16

Yippee! Third assignment completed, handed in, and returned with a pass. I am so pleased with myself, I made sure that I took loads of notes in the support session, and even asked for clarification on one point. I then sat down the same evening to get my first draft down, luckily I didn't have to prepare a lesson that evening, otherwise things might have been very different! I read the rubric carefully, highlighting parts as I went through, and made sure I knew exactly what to do, and then just wrote. At the weekend, I sat down and checked it through again, there was loads I needed to change, but, at least I had something to work from. The tutor made some really nice comments. Well chuffed!

Chilled-out Charlie: Day 16

LL: All right, mate? You don't look very happy.

CC: I'm not! I can't believe it; I've got to resubmit written assignment three. I thought I had this one in the bag but as it turns out, I missed out quite a large chunk of it!

LL: How did you manage that?

CC: I'm not sure, but Fastidious Felicity mentioned something about a checklist, perhaps I should have looked at that! It seems that just being able to write one thousand words isn't enough; you have to actually know what you're talking about! We've got written assignment support for the fourth one tomorrow, I'm going to listen to everything we're told, and then get cracking on it asap, so I don't forget what we've got to do.

LL: Fancy going out for a beer later?

CC: Nah, I'd better not, gotta do this resubmission.

The written assignment support sessions are for your benefit, and should be taken seriously. Make notes, and ask questions as necessary. The support sessions are timetabled to give you as much time as possible to complete the assignment, don't leave it till the last minute to start getting something on paper, instead get your first draft done as soon as time allows, while the support session is fresh in your mind. Read the rubric through carefully, and make sure you are covering all parts of the task.

Checklist

☑ Have I stuck to the word limit?

☑ Have I referenced my sources?

☑ Have I answered all parts of the question?

☑ Have I backed up with examples when required?

☑ Have I checked for spelling mistakes?

☑ Have I explained classroom activities clearly enough and included handouts, if necessary?

☑ Have I followed the format suggested by the tutor? If not, is the format I have chosen easy to follow?

Observation of Experienced Teachers

It's Wednesday evening, and Harassed Henry and Fastidious Felicity are observing Experienced Edith teaching a group of 8 intermediate students. Harassed Henry didn't have time to get anything to eat, as he had to dash home to take the dog for a walk before coming back to school, so he grabs a sandwich to eat while he's observing the lesson.

Fastidious Felicity's looking forward to watching a live lesson, she's heard that Experienced Edith is a really good teacher, and she hopes she'll be able to have a chat with some of the students too.

Harassed Henry arrives a couple of minutes after the lesson starts, but a couple of students are also late, so he hopes he isn't causing too much disruption. He sits down at the back of the class, and rummages through his bag looking for his observation tasks; they must be in there somewhere. Although he hasn't had time to look at the tasks yet, he's sure it can't be anything too much to do. He manages to find the task, starts to look for a pen, then tries to quietly unwrap his sandwich. A couple of students turn round and the teacher frowns - oh dear, not a good start!

Fastidious Felicity watches the lesson with interest, although secretly she thinks Experienced Edith isn't that great after all. She's pleased when one of the students turns round to ask her why the present perfect is used in the text, and even more pleased with herself that she can answer the question, experienced Edith is busy after all.

Harassed Henry: Day 18

Oh dear, I thought I'd got better at getting myself organised, but I seem to have reverted to type today. I was observing Experienced  Edith tonight, but, unfortunately, turned up late, which didn't really look very professional. I thought I could just sneak in and sit down quietly, but I then spent ages trying to find the observation task and something to write with. I felt terrible, because I know what it feels like to be disturbed while you're teaching. I made it even worse by tucking in to my sandwich but I was so hungry I couldn't wait!

Anyway, once I'd settled down, I got a lot out of the observation. It's really interesting to see a professional in action, everything that our tutors have been banging on about just came naturally to Experienced Edith. She always had the class's attention when she wanted it, her whiteboard was well-organised and she kept her TTT to an absolute minimum. It was a very student-centred lesson. I don't think Fastidious Felicity was quite as impressed as I was, but, when I reminded her that we all have different styles, she did accept that Experienced Edith was good at what she did. Right, best go and see if Pleasant Pat has managed to get the kids to bed.

Fastidious Felicity: Day 18

Well, I feel even better about my own teaching now. We observed Experienced Edith this evening, but I wasn't that impressed. She was good, but I was expecting fantastic, so was a little bit disappointed. As Harassed Henry pointed out once we'd got out of earshot, all teachers have different styles, and some might be more effective than others. I've learned a lot tonight though, there are some things you can only see the benefit of when you observe others doing it.

Experienced Edith did a lot of drilling with the students, and they really benefitted from it. I've always *seen drilling as a bit of an embarrassment, for both me and the students, but it seems that it is actually quite useful and the students seemed to really enjoy it!*

Right, best get on, I need to check that my materials are all in order for tomorrow.

Six hours of observation of experienced teachers is another important component of the course. Up to 3 hours of this can be observed on DVD, and the rest will be live teachers. This could take place outside course hours, depending on the centre. You'll be given observation tasks to complete during this time, which will help you with written assignments, as well as helping you with your own teaching. The centre will try to ensure you watch a good quality lesson, but, remember, watching a "bad" lesson can be as beneficial as a good one.

Checklist

- ☑ Have I got my CELTA 5 with me for the experienced teacher to sign?

- ☑ Have I left enough time to get to the classroom in plenty of time?

- ☑ Have I got the observation task(s)?

The Final Day

It's the final day of the course and the trainees have taught a full six hours of assessed lessons, completed all four written assignments, and observed six hours' worth of lessons delivered by experienced teachers. All that is left for them to do is have their CELTA 5 signed off by their tutor. They don't yet know what their final grade is, as the tutors still have to agree on grades with the external assessor, but they can look forward to receiving a provisional grade in the post fairly soon. The tutor is not allowed to tell the trainees whether they have passed the course or not but they do know that if they were in danger of failing the course, they would have been given **an extra** tutorial, this is not the case for Fastidious Felicity, Anxious Annie, Harassed Henry or Chilled-out Charlie so they are all feeling pretty pleased with themselves.

Anxious Annie doesn't want to waste any time and would like to start teaching as soon as possible, otherwise she might lose her nerve, so she is pleased that there is an input session on how to get a job and professional development. The trainer tells the trainees about private language schools which are always taking on new teachers and Anxious Annie makes a note of contact details so that she can send her CV out straight away. Interestingly, the tutor also discusses further training options such as Delta. Harassed Henry is looking forward to a couple of weeks off to spend some quality time with his family but makes some notes for future reference. Chilled-out Charlie will be returning to the classes he was teaching before the course, but is interested to find out about other opportunities which have opened up to him now that he has completed the CELTA course. He's quite excited at the thought of being able to get work anywhere in the world and is already thinking about packing his bags and heading somewhere new.

Anxious Annie: Day 20

I can't believe it's all over. What a roller-coaster the last four weeks have been, it's felt more like four months. I feel like I've really managed to change, and develop as an individual, and I've got so much more confidence than I had before the course started. I actually think that I'm quite a good teacher now. Sure, there are still some things I need to work on, but I can't wait to get started on my new career!

We had an input session today where the tutor told us about schools in the area which are always taking on newly qualified teachers so I'm going to get my CV sent out to them this weekend, there's no point in me hanging around. She also talked about Delta, don't think that's for me though- can't imagine signing up to do more observed teaching ever again! It's just too nerve-wracking! It sounds right up Fastidious Felicity's street though.

Although my tutor wasn't allowed to say anything, I

know I've passed the course, if I'd failed I would have been given an extra tutorial and I wasn't. Apparently, we'll be given a detailed report which we can send to prospective employers, I wonder what they'll say on mine "started off nervously and finished off not so nervously" lol!

Off out now, we're all meeting up for a celebration tonight. I've already had a couple of glasses of champagne so I'd better not drink much more ......

Trainee Diary Entries – Day 21

Fastidious Felicity

So, that's it. The course is over, and I've got the worst hangover ever. We had a great night last night, all of the trainees and tutors went for dinner and some drinks to celebrate the end of the course. Chilled-out Charlie was hilarious, he was really good at impersonating all of the tutors - they seemed to take it well though! Anxious Annie was also lots of fun. We went to a karaoke bar, and she got up and sang "I did it my way". She's a really good singer, but I doubt she would have done that before the course, she really has come out of her shell. I had a lovely chat with Harassed Henry, he told me how much he is looking forward to this next chapter in his life - he can't wait to be able to balance his time more , and spend more of it with his kids.

Chilled-out Charlie

CC: Well, I never thought an evening with the others would be so much fun, bet you're glad you joined us in the end, aren't you?

LL: You can always tell it's gonna be a good night when you get started on the impressions, and they really were up to standard, mate.

CC: And what about Anxious Annie knocking the tequilas back? Bet she's got a sore head today!

LL: She's a fantastic singer!

CC: There's no way she would've done that a few weeks ago, I think this course has changed us all.

LL: Has Fastidious Felicity changed? She seemed pretty fastidious about drinking that wine!

CC: She was great wasn't she? Was she how you expected?

LL: Yes, but in a good way, I only wish I could have focused on her positives, if you get my drift!

CC: Watch it! You've met Jolly John - I wouldn't want to mess with him!

LL: What're you doin' today?

CC: Well, I'm not teaching till Monday evening so I plan to do nothing this weekend except relax, catch up with some mates and watch some sport. I think I've got withdrawal symptoms - the course hasn't changed me that much! Fancy a drink? My head is pounding!

Harassed Henry

Oh dear, my head hurts! I should never have had that whisky Chilled-out Charlie persuaded me to have.

I can't believe it's all over. I'm really going to miss my fellow trainees; I hope we stay in touch. We had a great night last night. We all went out for drinks and dinner, and then went to a karaoke bar. While in the restaurant, Chilled-out Charlie started doing impersonations of the tutors, they were spot on, and really funny. He wasn't being malicious so it didn't matter that the tutors saw him! The best moment of the night, though, was when Anxious Annie got up, and sang "I did it my way" in the karaoke bar. She's a really good singer. I bet she wouldn't have done that pre-CELTA! I had a lovely chat with Fastidious Felicity; she's such a nice girl. We talked about what we're going to do now; she's already been offered a job at one of the private language schools in town, and will send me their contact details. I'm in no rush to fill up my week, but I will definitely get myself a few hours to start with - I mustn't forget that work/life balance is my goal, and that the kids take precedence.

Anxious Annie

We all went out to celebrate last night. Chilled-out Charlie certainly is an entertainer! He even managed to get me up to do karaoke. I've never done it before. It's something that I've always secretly wanted to do, and watched jealously when other friends have had the confidence to just get up there and sing, even if they're really bad! Well, last night, I was the one up on the stage.

The course has had such highs and lows. I've made some really good friends, and have achieved things (including karaoke!) that I never knew I was capable of. I really am quite proud of myself.

Five Years Later

Harassed Henry

So, five years eh? Has it really been that long? The time's flown by and my life has changed so much. I'm not sure where to start really.

After the CELTA course had finished I felt a bit deflated. It'd been such an intensive month, I found it difficult to adapt. It wasn't long before Pleasant Pat started nagging me to go out and find some work, she was right though I really did need to get started otherwise I would have got stuck in a rut again.

My first teaching job was for a small, private language school. I'll never forget that first lesson because it was a disaster. Everything I'd learned in those four weeks seemed to just go out the window, I was so glad I wasn't being observed! I was teaching a group of elementary students, there were about 12 of them from all over the place. I taught food items, you know the sort of thing – vegetables, fruit, types of meat and so on. This Japanese girl, Kaori I think her name was, kept asking me about *males*. She asked me "You go with wife to males?" and she was really insistent on getting an answer from me. The other students all looked like they thought it was a perfectly reasonable question but I found myself getting quite angry - how dare she suggest that my wife and I might be a bit kinky?! Unfortunately, it wasn't until I taught an upper-intermediate class a few months later and had another Japanese student who I told this problem to, that I finally realized what she meant. He also couldn't understand my problem with the question, except he was able to correct it slightly to "Do you go with your wife for males?" It then dawned on me that she was just struggling with the pronunciation of *meals*. Haha, still makes me laugh when I think about it.

Nowadays, I'm working at a college teaching English to asylum seekers. I love it, it's so rewarding. I teach a few different classes, from beginner upwards, some of the students have been with me from the beginning, when they could barely speak a word. They are so motivated and great fun to teach, amazing really given some of their backgrounds.

I think the best thing about my change of direction though is that ever since leaving my old job and completing the CELTA course, I have never felt bored with life. I spend so much more quality time with the kids and Pleasant Pat gets to do more for herself now that I am able to help out more at home.

I'm still in touch with the others, Anxious Annie and Pleasant Pat have become really good friends, they do Zumba together every Wednesday. Fastidious Felicity and I email occasionally and Chilled-out Charlie keeps us all up-to-date via Facebook, I'm not sure where he is at the moment - that bloke can't stay anywhere for long. I still think back fondly to our last night together - happy times.

Anxious Annie

What am I doing now? What aren't I doing? I am so busy at the moment, I don't know whether I'm coming or going.

As soon as the CELTA course came to an end, I sent my CV to all the schools within a 20-mile radius and thankfully got a few jobs out of it. The CELTA certificate really was what the schools were looking for. My first class came from one school that received my CV on the Friday morning, asked me to come in on the Friday afternoon and gave me a class starting immediately. I was soooo nervous before that first lesson, I couldn't sleep all weekend for worry but of course there was nothing to worry about. The students were lovely and when they asked me how long I'd been teaching, I was honest and told them it was my first lesson as a qualified teacher, they looked really surprised as if they thought I'd been doing it for years. I still see some of those students today.

I decided to go down the freelance route because I wanted to get experience from a few different places so I slowly built up my own timetable. I now teach in one private language school, have a couple of classes a week with pre-school kids and teach a couple of one-to-ones and groups in a car manufacturing company. I love that I could be singing nursery rhymes in the morning and writing business emails in the afternoon!

I guess the major thing for me though is that I have just completed Delta Module Three. I did Module One about two years after my CELTA course and really enjoyed it, there was no practical teaching, but I had to take an exam which was challenging and really made me read a lot. I passed Module One with a merit and my tutor encouraged me to go straight on to do Module Two. I was really worried about this one though; I was once again having to write assignments, detailed lesson plans and being observed. Needless to say, I got extremely nervous every time I was assessed but I'm pleased to say that I got through it. Module Three has been my favourite module, I chose option two, "English Language Teaching Management" but I think I would have also enjoyed Option One, "Extending Practice and ELT Specialism". Now that I have a Delta certificate I am seriously considering becoming a CELTA trainer. My tutor from when I did my CELTA is still at the centre and didn't laugh hysterically when I asked if she thought it might be possible so watch this space!

I'm still in touch with everyone, Fastidious Felicity and I get together once or twice a year and normally end up talking shop. I regularly meet up with Harrassed Henry's wife, Pleasant Pat, we've become quite close friends and do a Zumba class together once a week. Harrassed Henry makes me laugh with his stories about funny mistakes his students make and misunderstandings he has with them. Chilled-out Charlie is in Costa Rica I think. Apparently he's fallen for a local girl, I can't see him ever settling down though. I bumped into his mate Laid-back Larry last week, he asked me if I'm still doing it my way, I didn't have a clue what he was on about then he reminded me of that night on the karaoke! So funny, I'd forgotten all about it.

Chilled-out Charlie

CC:	All right mate? Can you hear me?
LL:	Yes, but I can't see you! Switch the video on.
CC:	Whoops, sorry - can you see me now?
LL:	Hiya, finally! Where are you?
CC:	In an Internet cafe in San José
LL:	What time is it there?
CC:	I dunno, about six.
LL :	In the morning?
CC:	No, evening. I'm just about to meet Sassy Savannah for a beer.
LL:	Who's Sassy Savannah? Where'd you meet her?
CC:	At the school I'm teaching at.
LL:	So you found some work then?
CC:	Yeah, dead easy. There's loads of work here. I nearly took a job in a call centre but then this teaching job came up so I'm happy.
LL:	How long do you reckon you'll stay in Costa Rica?
CC:	Well I really like this girl so I'll see how it goes.
LL:	Do you think you'll ever come home?
CC:	Dunno, I've been on the road for so long now I'm not sure how I would cope with being back home.
LL:	Aren't you homesick?
CC:	Not really, but I'm really missing Marmite!
LL:	Can't you get it there? Shall I send you some?
CC:	They only eat rice and beans here! Could you? That'd be great.
LL:	By the way, guess who I bumped into last

week.

CC: Who? Not my mum?

LL: No, that girl who did the karaoke on your CELTA course. What was her name?

CC: Oh Anxious Annie! Did you speak to her? How is she? Did she pass her Delta?

LL: What? I don't know, we only had a quick chat, she asked about you.

CC: It's been a while since I updated my status on Facebook.

LL: Is wotsit on Facebook?

CC: Who? Fastidious Felicity? Yeah, all my CELTA pals are

LL: She ever ask about me?

CC: Sorry to have to be the one to break it to you, but no!

LL: Shame!

CC: You really fancied her didn't you?!

LL: Yes!

SS: Hola querido!

CC: Oh hi! You're early. I'm just chatting to Laid-back Larry, my mate from back home.

SS: Hola Laid-back Larry! Nice to meet you

LL: Er, oh, uh, hello.

CC: OK mate, we're gonna go and have a beer now. I'll message you for a chat next week some time. See ya! Oh, and put your tongue away!

LL: Er, uh, yeah, right, see ya mate!

SS: Your friend is weird, no?

CC: Don't mind him babe, he doesn't get out much!

Fastidious Felicity

Well I have to say, the last five years haven't turned out quite as I had planned! After the CELTA course finished, I thought I would be able to start on the wedding preparations as well as my new career.

I got some work straightaway; a couple of the language schools were very impressed with me and offered me some courses starting immediately. One of the classes I was offered was an advanced conversation class. There were only 5 people in the group and very often Sexy Sergio was the only one who turned up, the others were regularly away on business. This meant that Sexy Sergio and I spent hours chatting, we sometimes went on to the pub or for a coffee after the course, one thing led to another and we ended up falling for each other! Poor Jolly John, I felt so sorry for him when I broke it to him but we're actually quite good friends now and we both realise it wouldn't really have worked; I need someone with a bit more oomph!

After a couple of years, Sexy Sergio decided he wanted to go back to his hometown, Porto, so that's where we've ended up. I threw myself into learning Portuguese, am now fluent and the beauty of having CELTA meant I could easily get work- there's such a demand for qualified EFL teachers here. I'm now setting up my own language school with a colleague, Energetic Ellie - we make a really good team. I never would have thought that my life would end up like this; I thought I'd be married to Jolly John with 2.4 children and doing two evenings work a week just to keep my hand in!

Anxious Annie comes to Portugal for a holiday most summers and might come out to run some summer courses once the school is up and running. Can't believe she's actually going to be a CELTA tutor! Who'd have thought it after seeing her at the beginning of our course! We all hear sporadically from Chilled-out Charlie but he never was the most reliable! I think back to those days with fond memories, I really changed as a result of that course, think I must've been a bit of a nightmare before - it certainly was a steep learning curve but well worth all the hard graft. Right must go and write a to-do list for the school opening!

Glossary

Aims
A section of the lesson plan that states what the teacher aims to do in the lesson.

CCQ
Concept Checking Question
A question that checks whether students have understood something the teacher has just introduced, whether it's grammar or lexis.

CELTA
Certificate of English Language Teaching to Adults.

CELTA 5
Candidate Record Booklet to be kept up to date throughout the course.

Contact hours
The number of hours spent at the centre.

Controlled practice
An activity in which the students' output is controlled by the teacher.

Cuisenaire rods
Small coloured wooden blocks, often used for teaching maths, which can be used in the EFL (English as a foreign language) classroom.

Delta Module 1	A written exam testing participants' understanding of language, methodology and resources for teaching.
Delta Module 2	Written assignments and observed teaching practice (TP).
Delta Module 3	An extended assignment on the participants' chosen specialism eg. Teaching one-to-one.
Drilling	The teacher models a word or phrase and then the students repeat it. This can be done chorally or individually or both.
EFL	English as a foreign language
ELT	English Language Teaching.
Finger correction	The teacher uses her fingers to indicate where a student has made a mistake.
Freer practice	An activity in which students have more free choice in what they produce.
ICQ	**Instruction Checking Question** A questioning technique used in teaching that checks whether

students have understood what
they need to do.

**Language
analysis**   A section on the lesson plan which
looks at the use, form and
phonology of the language.

Lexis   The vocabulary of a language.

Materials   What the teacher uses in the
classroom, for example pages from
a coursebook or flashcards.

NTS   **Not to standard**
The grade given if your lesson is
not good enough for the stage of
the course.

Peer-correction   When one student corrects
another.

Phonology   The sound system of a language.

Portfolio   A folder which contains a trainee's
lesson plans, materials, self
evaluations, feedback from the
tutor and written assignments.

**Post-fluency
feedback**   Feedback after an activity in which
students were focussing on
speaking fluently rather than
accurately.

Pre-course task   A task trainees are given to do before the course begins to help them with their language awareness.

Procedure   The part of the lesson plan which tells the teacher what to do in each part of the lesson.

Rubric   The instructions for the written assignment.

Self-correction   When a student corrects himself.

Self-evaluation   After every session of teaching practice (TP), trainees complete a written analysis and reflection of their lesson.

Skills   The four key skills of language use: reading, listening, speaking and writing

STT   **Student Talking Time**
The amount the students talk in the lesson.

Sub-skills   Sub-skills are skills relating to one of the four key skills and are employed depending on the language aim. Some examples of sub-skills are skimming and scanning (key skill = reading) or listening for gist (key skill = listening)

TD Aim **Teaching Development Aim**
A personal aim that you write on your lesson plan. Something that you aim to work on in your lesson.

TP **Teaching Practice**
There are 6 hours of assessed teaching practice on the course.

TP group **Teaching Practice Group**
A group of max 6 trainees. Trainees work in this group for TP planning, TP & TP feedback.

TP points **Teaching Practice Points**
The information/help trainees are given before each TP. In these points, the trainees are advised what to teach and possibly how to teach it.

TS **To Standard**
The grade given if your lesson is standard for the stage of the course.

TS+
To Standard Plus
The highest grade a trainee can receive for TP, awarded if the lesson is above standard for the stage of the course.

TTT
Teacher Talking Time
The amount the teacher talks in the lesson.

WA support
Written Assignment Support
A support session for each written assignment to help them prepare for the task.

The Ultimate Guide to CELTA

Amanda Momeni & Emma Jones

ultimateguidetocelta@gmail.com

15094975R00071

Printed in Poland
by Amazon Fulfillment
Poland Sp. z o.o., Wrocław